Reflective Exercises The International Experiences Guide

Reflective Exercises The International Experiences Guide

Empowering Your Journey Abroad

Brandon Arroues, M.Ed.

Brilliant Consulting

CONTENTS

Dedication

This workbook is dedicated to the courageous and adventurous individuals who dare to step out of their comfort zones to experience our global communities. Your journeys inspire and pave the way for future explorers.

Author's Note

Thank you to all the international students and educational professionals who shared their experiences and insights, making this guide a valuable resource for future generations of students embarking on their own global adventures. Drawing on my own diverse global experiences, and the thought-provoking wisdom shared by others, I began the arduous task of writing this comprehensive guide and workbook. I hope it may encourage, support, and guide you through your amazing journey as you prepare to embark on your next international adventure.

Welcome to "**Reflective Exercises: The International Experiences Guide Workbook**," your essential companion to "International Experiences: A Comprehensive Guide." This workbook is designed to help you internalize the insights and strategies presented in the primary guide, offering a hands-on approach to navigating the complexities of life abroad. By engaging with these exercises, you'll be better equipped to adapt to your new environment, overcome challenges, and make the most of your international experience.

Purpose of the Workbook

Living abroad is an exciting journey filled with opportunities for personal growth, cultural immersion, and academic achievement. However, it also comes with its share of challenges. This workbook aims to provide you with practical tools and reflective exercises that complement the comprehensive guidance provided in "International Experiences: A Comprehensive Guide." Through this structured approach, you will:

- **Internalize Key Concepts**: Deepen your understanding of cultural adaptation, coping with culture shock, and building support networks.
- **Apply Learnings**: Translate theoretical knowledge into actionable steps tailored to your personal experiences and goals.
- **Enhance Self-Awareness**: Reflect on your journey, recognize your progress, and identify areas for further growth.

Structure of the Workbook

The workbook is organized to mirror the chapters of the primary guide, providing targeted exercises and reflective questions that align with the content of each chapter. Here's what you can expect:

Reflective Exercises: Each chapter begins with exercises designed to help you reflect on your personal experiences and internalize the concepts discussed in the guide.

Action Plans: Develop concrete plans for applying the strategies you've learned, tailored to your unique situation and goals.

Continuous Learning: Engage in activities that promote ongoing reflection and adaptation, ensuring you remain resilient and open-minded throughout your journey.

How to Use This Workbook

This workbook is a flexible tool designed to support you at every stage of your international journey. Here are some tips on how to make the most of it:

Regular Engagement: Set aside dedicated time each week to work through the exercises. Consistent reflection and planning will help you stay on track and adapt more effectively.

Personalization: Tailor the exercises to your personal experiences and needs. The more specific and honest you are, the more beneficial the reflections will be.

Collaboration: Share your reflections and action plans with peers, mentors, or support networks. Collaborative discussions can provide additional insights and encouragement.

Review and Revise: Periodically review your reflections and plans. Adjust them as needed to reflect your evolving experiences and goals.

Benefits of Reflective Practice

Engaging in reflective practice through this workbook offers numerous benefits:

Enhanced Adaptability: By regularly reflecting on your experiences and challenges, you develop a greater ability to adapt to new situations and environments.

Deeper Cultural Understanding: Reflective exercises encourage you to delve deeper into the cultural nuances of your host country, fostering a richer and more meaningful exchange experience.

Personal Growth: Self-reflection promotes personal growth by helping you understand your strengths, areas for improvement, and the impact of your experiences on your overall development.

Final Thoughts

As you embark on this exciting journey, remember that every experience, whether positive or challenging, contributes to your growth and learning. "Reflective Exercises: The International Experiences Guide Workbook" is here to support you every step of the way, providing a structured approach to navigating the complexities of studying abroad.

Embrace this opportunity with an open mind and a willingness to learn. Use this workbook as a tool to reflect on your experiences, set meaningful goals, and develop strategies to thrive in your new environment.

The insights and skills you gain through this process will not only enhance your international experience but also equip you with valuable competencies for your future endeavors.

Welcome to a journey of discovery, growth, and global learning. Safe travels, and may your time abroad be enriching and transformative!

Chapter 1: Preparing for Your Journey

These reflective exercises and questions are designed to help you internalize the content of Chapter 1, apply it to your personal situation, and deepen your learning experience. Engaging with these activities will not only prepare you for your journey but also enhance your overall exchange experience.

Exercise 1: Personal Preparation Plan

Objective: To create a comprehensive, personalized plan for preparing for your exchange experience.

Instructions:

1. **Travel Arrangements:**
    - List all the steps you need to take to book your flights, including researching options, comparing prices, and considering student discounts.
    - Create a timeline for booking your flight. When will you start looking for tickets? When do you plan to purchase them?
2. **Visa and Immigration:**
    - Research the specific visa requirements for your host country.
    - List the documents you need to gather for your visa application.
    - Create a checklist and timeline for completing your visa application. When will you gather each document? When do you plan to submit your application?

3. **Financial Planning:**
   - Outline your estimated expenses, including tuition, housing, food, transportation, and personal spending.
   - Identify potential sources of funding, such as scholarships, part-time work, or financial aid.
   - Create a budget that details your expected income and expenses. How will you manage your finances to ensure you stay within your budget?

Carlos's Story: Navigating the Visa Application Process

Carlos, a business student from Brazil, was excited about his upcoming exchange program in Canada. However, he quickly realized that the visa application process was more complex than anticipated. "I thought getting a visa would be straightforward, but it turned out to be a detailed and time-consuming task. I had to gather numerous documents, including financial statements, health records, and an acceptance letter from my host university."

Despite the challenges, Carlos found that staying organized made a significant difference. "I created a folder on my computer and a physical binder to keep track of all the documents. I also set reminders for important deadlines and double-checked the requirements regularly."

Expert Insight: Carlos's experience underscores the importance of thorough preparation for the visa application process. Understanding the specific requirements of your host country and starting the process early can mitigate stress. Keeping a checklist of necessary documents and deadlines ensures nothing is overlooked. Additionally, using both digital and physical organization methods can help manage the paperwork more efficiently.

Actionable Tip: Begin your visa application process as soon as you receive your acceptance letter. Create a detailed checklist of required documents and deadlines. Use both digital tools (like reminder apps and cloud storage) and physical methods (like binders and folders) to keep your paperwork organized. Regularly check the embassy or consulate website for any updates or additional requirements.

Reflection Questions:

How does creating a detailed plan help reduce your anxiety about the upcoming exchange?

_____

_____

_____

_____

_____

_____

What challenges do you anticipate in the preparation process, and how can you address them proactively?

_____

_____

_____

_____

_____

_____

Emma's Story: Packing Wisely for a Year Abroad

Emma, an engineering student from the UK, had a mixed experience packing for her year-long stay in Australia. "I packed way too many clothes and ended up not using half of them. I also forgot some essentials like a power adapter and my favorite snacks from home. It was a hassle trying to find replacements in a new country."

Emma learned from her initial packing mistakes and adapted quickly. "I started talking to other international students who had been in Australia longer. They gave me great tips on what was actually useful to bring and what I could easily buy there. I also joined a local community group online, which helped me understand what I really needed."

Expert Insight: Emma's story highlights the importance of strategic packing. Focus on essentials and versatile clothing that can be layered. Remember to account for the climate of your host country and any specific items you might not easily find abroad. Connecting with experienced international students or local community groups can provide valuable insights into what to bring and what to buy locally.

Actionable Tip: Make a packing list that includes essential documents, medications, and versatile clothing. Research the climate and local stores in your host country to determine what you can purchase after arrival. Join online communities or forums related to your host country for packing advice. Don't forget adapters and any specific items from home that you might miss, like favorite snacks or personal care products.

Reflection Questions:

How can you stay flexible and adapt your plan if unexpected changes arise?

_____

_____

_____

_____

_____

_____

Exercise 2: Visualization and Goal Setting

Objective: To visualize your exchange experience and set meaningful goals that align with your personal and academic aspirations.

Instructions:

1. **Visualization:**
   ◦ Close your eyes and imagine your first day in your host country. What do you see, hear, and feel?
   ◦ Visualize your daily routine. Where will you live? How will you commute to school? What will your classes be like?
2. **Goal Setting:**
   ◦ Write down three personal goals you want to achieve during your exchange. These could relate to personal growth, cultural immersion, or building new relationships.
   ◦ Write down three academic goals you want to achieve. Consider goals related to your coursework, academic performance, or learning new skills.
   ◦ For each goal, list the steps you need to take to achieve it. How will you measure your progress?

Jin's Story: Managing Financial Preparations

Jin, an economics student from South Korea, faced unexpected financial challenges during his exchange in the United States. "I underestimated the cost of living and had to find a part-time job to make ends meet. Luckily, my university had resources to help international students find employment. I also found budgeting apps to be incredibly useful in managing my finances."

Jin's proactive approach to financial management paid off. "I attended a financial planning workshop at my university, which taught me how to create a detailed budget and find cost-saving opportunities. I also learned about scholarships and grants that I hadn't initially considered. These resources were lifesavers."

Expert Insight: Jin's experience emphasizes the necessity of comprehensive financial planning. Researching the cost of living in your host country and creating a detailed budget can prevent financial strain. Exploring all available scholarships, grants, and employment opportunities before departure is crucial. Using budgeting apps and attending financial planning workshops can provide additional support.

Actionable Tip: Create a detailed budget that includes tuition, housing, food, transportation, and personal expenses. Look into scholarships, grants, and part-time job opportunities well before your departure. Use budgeting apps to track your spending and identify areas where you can save money. Attend financial planning workshops or seek advice from your university's financial aid office. Set up an emergency fund to cover any unexpected expenses.

Reflection Questions:

How do your goals reflect your personal values and aspirations?

_____

_____

_____

_____

_____

_____

What resources or support will you need to achieve your goals?

_____

_____

_____

_____

_____

Sara's Story: Preparing for Health and Safety

Sara, a medical student from Spain, was excited about her exchange program in South Africa but was concerned about health and safety. "I knew I needed certain vaccinations and wanted to ensure I had access to healthcare if needed. I also wanted to understand the local safety guidelines."

Sara took proactive steps to address her concerns. "I visited a travel health clinic well before my departure to get the necessary vaccinations and advice on staying healthy abroad. I also researched health insurance options to find a plan that covered me comprehensively. Additionally, I attended a safety briefing organized by my home university, which provided valuable information on staying safe."

Expert Insight: Sara's approach underscores the importance of thorough preparation for health and safety. Visiting a travel health clinic to get vaccinations and health advice is crucial. Researching health insurance options ensures you have the necessary coverage. Attending safety briefings and familiarizing yourself with local safety guidelines can help you stay informed and prepared.

Actionable Tip: Visit a travel health clinic to get the necessary vaccinations and health advice for your destination. Research and purchase comprehensive health insurance that covers you during your stay. Attend safety briefings and familiarize yourself with local safety guidelines. Keep a list of emergency contacts, including local emergency numbers and your country's embassy or consulate.

Exercise 3: Cultural Research and Adaptation Plan

Objective: To research the culture of your host country and develop a plan for cultural adaptation.

Instructions:

1. **Cultural Research:**
   - Research the cultural norms, values, and etiquette of your host country. Consider aspects such as communication styles, social behaviors, and dining customs.
   - Identify three cultural differences that might impact your daily life. How do these differ from your home country?
2. **Adaptation Plan:**
   - Create a list of strategies for adapting to these cultural differences. How can you show respect and openness to the local culture?
   - Identify opportunities to immerse yourself in the local culture, such as attending cultural events, joining clubs, or making local friends.

Reflection Questions:

How can understanding cultural differences enhance your exchange experience?

_____

_____

_____

_____

_____

_____

What challenges do you anticipate in adapting to a new culture, and how can you prepare for them?

_____

_____

_____

_____

_____

_____

How can you balance maintaining your own cultural identity while respecting and integrating into your host culture?

_____
_____
_____
_____
_____
_____
_____

Exercise 4: Building a Support Network

Objective: To plan how to build a support network that will provide emotional and practical support during your exchange.

Instructions:

1. **Identify Potential Support:**
   - List the people and resources you can rely on for support in your host country, such as international student advisors, professors, classmates, and local friends.
   - Consider how you will stay connected with family and friends from home. What communication methods will you use?
2. **Action Plan:**
   - Develop a plan for building and maintaining your support network. How will you introduce yourself and build relationships with new contacts?
   - Identify strategies for seeking help when needed. How will you approach others for support in difficult times?

Liam's Story: Building a Support Network in Germany

Liam's exchange program took him to Berlin, where he was eager to immerse himself in the vibrant arts scene and rich history. Despite his enthusiasm, he found it challenging to connect with locals and other students initially.

"I joined a local soccer club, and that changed everything for me," Liam explained. "Playing soccer together broke down barriers and created instant connections. I also attended international student meetups, which were invaluable for making friends who understood the unique challenges we all faced."

Expert Insight: Liam's proactive approach to joining local groups and attending social events is a powerful strategy for building a support network. Engaging in activities you enjoy provides a natural setting for meeting people and forming bonds.

Actionable Tip: Identify clubs, organizations, or events that align with your interests. Whether it's sports, arts, or academic societies, these platforms offer excellent opportunities to meet like-minded individuals and establish a support system.

Reflection Questions:

How can a strong support network enhance your exchange experience?

_____
_____
_____
_____
_____
_____

What qualities do you look for in a supportive relationship?

_____
_____
_____
_____
_____
_____

How can you contribute to the support network of other exchange students?

_____
_____
_____
_____
_____
_____

Exercise 5: Reflective Journaling

Objective: To reflect on your thoughts, feelings, and experiences as you prepare for your exchange.

Instructions:

1. **Journaling Prompts:**
   ○ Describe your emotions as you prepare for your exchange. What excites you? What concerns you?

- Reflect on an experience where you faced a significant change or challenge. How did you cope with it? What did you learn from that experience that you can apply to your exchange?

2. **Regular Entries:**
   - Set aside time each week to write about your preparation progress. What have you accomplished? What obstacles have you encountered?
   - Reflect on your growth and learning throughout the preparation process. How are you changing and evolving as you get ready for this new chapter.

Reflection Questions:

How does journaling help you process your emotions and thoughts about the exchange?

_____

_____

_____

_____

_____

_____

What insights have you gained about yourself through this reflective practice?

_____

_____

_____

_____

_____

How can you use journaling as a tool for ongoing reflection during your exchange?

_____

_____

_____

_____

_____

Chapter 2: Navigating and Adapting to a New Cultural Environment

These reflective exercises and questions are designed to help you internalize the content from Chapter 2, apply it to your personal situation, and deepen your learning experience. Engage with these activities thoughtfully to enhance your adaptation process and maximize your international exchange experience.

Exercise 1: Personal Culture Shock Timeline

Objective: To recognize and map out your personal experiences with culture shock stages.

Instructions:

1. **Identify Stages:** Reflect on your initial days in the host country. Identify moments that correspond to the honeymoon, frustration, adjustment, and acceptance phases of culture shock.
2. **Map Your Experience:** Create a timeline marking significant events or feelings during each phase. Include dates and brief descriptions.
3. **Reflection:** Write a short paragraph about each phase, focusing on what you felt and how you managed those feelings.

Maria's Story: Overcoming Culture Shock in Japan

When Maria arrived in Tokyo, she was immediately captivated by the bustling streets, neon lights, and the politeness of the people. However, after the initial excitement wore off, she began to feel overwhelmed by the language barrier and the cultural differences. Simple tasks like grocery shopping or using public transportation became daunting challenges.

Maria shared, "I remember feeling completely lost during my first week. The signs were in Japanese, and I struggled to communicate even the most basic needs. It was frustrating and isolating."

Expert Insight: Maria's experience highlights the common initial excitement followed by frustration—a typical progression of culture shock. To manage these feelings, it's important to prepare by learning some basic phrases and familiarizing yourself with common signs and symbols in the local language. Carrying a phrasebook or using translation apps can be extremely helpful.

Actionable Tip: Set small, achievable goals each day, like learning a new phrase or successfully completing a specific task. Celebrate these small victories to boost your confidence and gradually build your comfort level in the new environment.

Reflection Questions:

How did your initial excitement about the new culture manifest?

_____

_____

_____

_____

_____

_____

What were the main challenges you might face during the frustration phase, and how will you cope with them?

_____

_____

_____

_____

_____

_____

What routines or strategies might help you transition into the adjustment phase?

_____

_____

_____

_____

_____

_____

At what point should you feel a sense of acceptance and integration into the new culture?

_____

_____

_____

_____

Aisha's Story: Embracing Cultural Differences in Brazil

Aisha traveled to São Paulo with an open mind and a curiosity about Brazilian culture. She quickly realized that her usual approach to social interactions didn't always align with local customs.

"I had to get used to the warm and expressive communication style," she recalled. "In Brazil, people are very affectionate and use a lot of physical contact, which was quite different from what I was used to. At first, it felt uncomfortable, but I learned to appreciate and reciprocate this warmth."

Expert Insight: Aisha's experience underscores the importance of cultural sensitivity and open-mindedness. Adapting to different social norms and communication styles is crucial for successful cultural integration. Observing and mimicking respectful behaviors can help ease this transition.

Actionable Tip: Take note of how locals interact in various situations and try to mirror these behaviors. This shows respect and willingness to integrate. If you're unsure about a particular custom, don't hesitate to ask for guidance from local friends or mentors.

Additional Insights:

- Consider creating a visual representation of your timeline using different colors for each phase. This can help you see your progression more clearly.
- Share your timeline with a peer or mentor to gain different perspectives on your experience and coping strategies.

Exercise 2: Building a Support Network Plan

Objective: To develop a strategy for building a robust support network in your host country.

Instructions:

1. **Identify Resources:** List potential resources for building your support network, including international student associations, local friends, mentors, and online communities.
2. **Action Steps:** Outline specific actions you will take to connect with these resources. For example, attending an international student welcome event, joining a local club, or participating in online forums.
3. **Goals:** Set three specific goals related to building your support network. For instance, "I will join two student clubs within the first month."

Carlos' Story: Coping with Homesickness in Canada

Carlos arrived in Vancouver excited to start his engineering program. However, he soon found himself missing his family and the familiar comforts of home. "The homesickness hit hard, especially during holidays and family events back home. It was tough, but I found ways to cope," he said.

Carlos stayed connected with his family through weekly video calls and joined a Latin American student association that hosted cultural events. "Being part of a community that shared my cultural background made a huge difference. It felt like a piece of home away from home."

Expert Insight: Homesickness is a common challenge for many international students. Staying connected with family and finding communities that share your cultural background can provide significant emotional support.

Actionable Tip: Establish a routine for staying in touch with loved ones, whether through regular video calls, social media, or messaging apps. Additionally, seek out cultural or national student groups that offer a sense of familiarity and belonging.

Reflection Questions:

Which local events or groups do you plan to join, and why?

_____

_____

_____

_____

_____

_____

How can connecting with other international students benefit your experience?

_____

_____

_____

_____

_____

_____

What steps will you take to build meaningful relationships with local residents?

_____

_____

_____

_____

_____

_____

Additional Insights:

- Consider scheduling regular check-ins with your support network to maintain strong connections.
- Reflect on how your support network can help you achieve your academic, personal, and cultural goals.

Exercise 3: Developing Cultural Sensitivity

Objective: To enhance your understanding and appreciation of cultural differences.

Instructions:

1. **Research:** Choose three aspects of your host culture that are significantly different from your own (e.g., greetings, dining etiquette, social behaviors). Research these aspects in detail.
2. **Observation:** Spend a week observing these cultural practices in action. Take notes on what you see and experience.
3. **Reflection:** Reflect on how these differences impact your interactions and understanding of the local culture. Write a brief essay summarizing your findings and reflections.

Reflection Questions:

How do the cultural norms you researched differ from those in your home country?

_____

_____

_____

_____

_____

_____

What surprised you about these cultural practices, and why?

_____

_____

_____

_____

_____

_____

How can understanding these differences improve your interactions with locals?

_____

_____

_____

_____

_____

_____

Additional Insights:

- Discuss your observations with a local friend or mentor to gain deeper insights into the cultural practices.
- Consider how your own cultural background influences your perceptions and interactions.

Exercise 4: Coping Strategies Journal

Objective: To develop and document effective coping strategies for managing culture shock.

Instructions:

1. **Identify Triggers**: Reflect on moments when you felt overwhelmed or homesick. Identify specific triggers (e.g., language barriers, social isolation, academic stress).
2. **Strategy Development**: For each trigger, develop a coping strategy. This might include mindfulness practices, seeking support from friends, or engaging in a favorite hobby.
3. **Daily Journal**: Keep a daily journal for two weeks, documenting any challenges you face and how you apply your coping strategies.

Reflection Questions:

What are the most common triggers of culture shock for you?

_____

_____

_____

_____

_____

Which coping strategies have been most effective in managing these triggers?

_____

_____

_____

_____

_____

_____

How will implementing these strategies make you feel, and what changes might you notice in your adjustment process?

_____

_____

_____

_____

_____

_____

Additional Insights:

- Share your journal entries with a trusted friend or mentor to receive feedback and additional coping suggestions.
- Revisit your journal entries periodically to track your progress and adjust your strategies as needed.

Exercise 5: Reflective Goal Setting

Objective: To set meaningful goals that support your cultural adaptation and personal growth.

Instructions:

1. **Goal Identification:** Identify three personal goals related to your cultural adaptation. These could be learning the local language, making local friends, or understanding cultural norms.
2. **Action Plan:** Create a detailed action plan for each goal, including specific steps, timelines, and resources needed.
3. **Reflection:** Write a reflection on why these goals are important to you and how achieving them will enhance your exchange experience.

Reflection Questions:

What are your top three goals for cultural adaptation, and why are they important to you?

_____
_____
_____
_____
_____
_____

What specific steps will you take to achieve each goal?

_____
_____
_____
_____
_____

How will you measure your progress and success in achieving these goals?

_____
_____
_____
_____
_____
_____

Additional Insights:

- Consider creating a vision board with images and quotes that represent your goals and keep you motivated.
- Set up regular progress reviews to celebrate achievements and adjust your action plans as necessary.

Exercise 6: Engaging in Cultural Exchange

Objective: To actively participate in cultural exchange activities and deepen your understanding of your host culture.

Instructions:

1. **Cultural Exchange Activities**: Identify cultural exchange activities you can participate in, such as language exchange programs, cooking classes, or cultural festivals.
2. **Participation Plan**: Develop a plan for participating in these activities. Include specific dates, locations, and any preparation needed.
3. **Reflection**: After participating in each activity, reflect on your experience and how it contributed to your understanding of the host culture.

Reflection Questions:

What cultural exchange activities are you most interested in, and why?

_____
_____
_____
_____
_____
_____

How do these activities help you connect with the local community?

_____
_____
_____
_____
_____
_____

What new insights or skills did you gain from participating in these activities?

_____
_____
_____
_____
_____
_____

Additional Insights:

- Share your cultural exchange experiences with your support network to inspire others to get involved.
- Reflect on how these activities have changed your perceptions and increased your cultural empathy.

Chapter 3: Settling In

Exercise 1: Finding the Perfect Accommodation

Objective: To help you identify and secure the best accommodation that meets your needs and preferences while ensuring safety and comfort.

Instructions:

1. Create a checklist of your ideal accommodation. Consider factors such as location, budget, amenities, and proximity to campus.
2. Use online resources to research three potential accommodation options in your host city. Note down the pros and cons of each option.
3. Visit or arrange virtual tours for these options, if possible, to get a better feel for the place and spot any potential issues.
4. Review the rental agreements carefully and, if needed, seek assistance from your university's housing office or a local contact.

Maria's Story: Finding a Place to Call Home

"When I first arrived in Barcelona, finding the right accommodation felt like a huge task. I didn't know where to start, and everything seemed so different from back home in Argentina. I started looking for private rentals online, but I quickly realized that visiting the places in person was crucial. After a few disappointments, I finally found a charming apartment close to the university. The landlord was kind enough to explain the rental agreement thoroughly, and I felt much more secure signing it. The key was starting early and being persistent."

Expert Insight: Maria's experience highlights the importance of starting your accommodation search well in advance. Use trusted rental websites and always try to visit properties in person if possible. This hands-on approach helps you get a better feel for the place and spot any potential issues. Understanding the local rental market and lease terms can prevent future headaches. Don't be afraid to ask for help from your university's housing office or local friends—they can provide invaluable advice.

Actionable Tip: Create a checklist of what you need in an accommodation, including proximity to campus, price range, and amenities. Start your search early, and if you can't visit in person, ask for a virtual tour. Having a trusted local contact review your lease agreement can also offer peace of mind.

Reflection Questions:

What are the top three priorities for you when choosing accommodation, and why?

_____
_____
_____
_____
_____
_____

How did your research help clarify your preferences and requirements for housing?

_____
_____
_____
_____
_____
_____

What challenges do you anticipate in securing accommodation, and how can you overcome them?

_____
_____
_____
_____
_____
_____

Additional Insights:

- Start your search well in advance to avoid last-minute stress.
- Utilize trusted websites and platforms recommended by your university or fellow students.
- Don't hesitate to ask for help from local contacts or university resources—they can provide valuable insights and help you avoid common pitfalls.

Exercise 2: Navigating Your New Environment

Objective: To familiarize yourself with the local transportation system and confidently navigate your new city.

Instructions:

1. Download a local transit app and explore the transportation routes to your university, grocery stores, and other key locations.
2. Plan a weekend outing using public transportation. Choose a destination you're excited about and map out your journey.
3. Practice using public transportation during less busy times to build your confidence.

Jens' Story: Mastering Public Transportation

"Moving from a small town in Denmark to New York City was a big change. The sheer size of the city and its transit system was overwhelming at first. But the university orientation included a detailed tour of the public transportation system, which was incredibly helpful. I downloaded a transit app recommended by a friend, which made navigating the subways much easier. Within a few weeks, I was exploring the city confidently, even finding shortcuts and less crowded routes."

Expert Insight: Jens's proactive approach to understanding the local transit system paid off. Participating in university orientation programs and using local transit apps are excellent strategies for mastering public transportation. These resources can help you become more independent and confident in navigating your new city. The more you explore, the more comfortable you'll feel.

Actionable Tip: Attend any transit tours or orientation sessions offered by your university. Download transit apps and explore local transportation websites to familiarize yourself with routes and schedules. Practice using public transportation during less busy times to build your confidence.

Reflection Questions:

What was the most challenging part of understanding the local transit system, and how did you address it?

_____

_____

_____

_____

_____

_____

How does familiarizing yourself with public transportation impact your confidence in navigating the city?

_____

_____

_____

_____

_____

_____

Describe your planned outing. What are you looking forward to the most, and why?

_____

_____

_____

_____

_____

_____

Additional Insights:

- Take advantage of any university-led orientation programs that include transit tours.
- Learning to navigate public transportation can save you money and reduce stress.
- Explore during off-peak hours first to get comfortable before trying peak travel times.

Exercise 3: Managing Daily Life

Objective: To establish a routine and manage daily tasks efficiently in your new environment.

Instructions:

1. Create a weekly schedule that includes academic commitments, grocery shopping, cooking, exercise, and leisure activities.
2. Identify local stores or markets where you can buy groceries and other essentials. Note any differences from what you're used to at home.
3. Set up a local bank account and mobile phone plan to simplify financial transactions and communication.

Amina's Story: Managing Daily Life in a New Culture

"Adjusting to life in Tokyo was both exciting and challenging. Grocery shopping was a bit confusing at first because I couldn't read the labels, but I joined a local cooking class which turned out to be a fantastic decision. Not only did I learn to cook traditional Japanese dishes, but I also made friends who helped me navigate other aspects of daily life. Opening a bank account was another hurdle, but the bank staff were incredibly helpful and patient, which made the process smooth."

Expert Insight: Amina's story underscores the value of engaging in local activities to better understand daily life in your new environment. Joining classes or groups can provide both practical skills and social connections. For tasks like banking, don't hesitate to seek assistance from staff who are often willing to help. These small steps can make your everyday life much easier and more enjoyable.

Actionable Tip: Look for community classes or groups that interest you. They can offer a great way to meet people and learn more about the local culture. When dealing with administrative tasks, always ask for help if you need it—local staff are usually happy to assist.

Reflection Questions:

How will your new weekly schedule compare to your routine back home? What adjustments will you need to make?

_____

_____

_____

_____

_____

_____

What strategies have you found effective for managing daily tasks and staying organized that you can apply in your new environment?

_____

_____

_____

_____

_____

_____

How will exploring local stores and markets enrich your experience of living in your host country?

_____

_____

_____

_____

_____

_____

Additional Insights:

- Prioritize creating a balanced schedule to ensure you have time for academics, socializing, and self-care.
- Exploring local markets can be a fun way to immerse yourself in the culture and discover new foods.
- Setting up local financial and communication services can streamline your daily life and help you feel more settled.

Exercise 4: Social Integration

Objective: To build a supportive social network and integrate into the local community.

Instructions:

1. Join at least one club or student organization at your university. Attend a meeting or event and take note of your experience.
2. Make a list of local cultural activities or festivals you'd like to attend. Plan to participate in at least one within the next month.
3. Actively engage with your new friends and acquaintances by organizing or joining social activities.

Carlos' Story: Building a Social Network

"When I arrived in Sydney, making friends was my top priority. Joining the international student association at my university was a game-changer. We had regular meetups, cultural nights, and even weekend trips. Additionally, I joined a local soccer team, which helped me meet locals and get a different perspective on life in Australia. These connections made my stay much more enjoyable and enriching."

Expert Insight: Carlos's efforts to build a social network by joining both international and local groups are commendable. Participating in university associations and local clubs can help you create a diverse social circle, providing support and a richer experience. Being proactive in social settings and open to new friendships can significantly enhance your exchange experience.

Actionable Tip: Join both international student groups and local clubs to broaden your social network. Attend events regularly and actively participate to build lasting friendships and connections.

Reflection Questions:

How can participating in a club or organization help you connect with others and feel more integrated into the campus community?

_____

_____

_____

_____

_____

_____

What cultural activity or festival are you most excited to attend, and what do you hope to learn from it?

_____

_____

_____

_____

_____

_____

Reflect on your interactions with your friends and acquaintances. What strategies have you used to build meaningful relationships? How can you apply those strategies in your global experiences?

_____

_____

_____

_____

_____

_____

Additional Insights:

- Joining clubs and attending events are excellent ways to meet people and build a sense of community.
- Participating in local cultural activities can provide deeper insights into your host country's traditions and way of life.
- Building a diverse social network can offer support and enrich your overall experience.

Exercise 5: Academic Success

Objective: To achieve academic success by utilizing university resources and developing effective study habits.

Instructions:

1. Set specific academic goals for the semester. Include both short-term and long-term objectives.
2. Identify three academic resources at your university (e.g., library, tutoring services, professor office hours) and describe how you plan to use them.
3. Create a study schedule that balances your coursework with other commitments.

Priya's Story: Thriving Academically

"Studying in Berlin was a unique experience. The academic culture was different from India, but I quickly adapted by making full use of campus resources. The library was a sanctuary, and I often joined study groups that improved my grasp of the coursework. I made it a habit to visit professors during office hours, which turned out to be incredibly beneficial. Their guidance helped me navigate the academic expectations and excel in my studies."

Expert Insight: Priya's proactive approach to academic success is commendable. Making the most of campus resources like libraries, study groups, and professor office hours can greatly enhance your understanding and performance. Building relationships with professors can provide additional support and insights into your coursework, making your academic journey smoother and more rewarding.

Actionable Tip: Make use of all available academic resources, including libraries and study groups. Regularly attend office hours to seek clarification and build rapport with your professors.

Reflection Questions:

What are your top academic goals for this semester, and why are they important to you?

_____
_____
_____
_____
_____
_____

How do the academic resources available at your school or university support your learning and success?

_____
_____
_____
_____
_____
_____

What steps can you take to actively engage with your professors and peers to enhance your academic experience?

_____
_____
_____
_____
_____
_____

Additional Insights:

- Regularly review and adjust your academic goals to stay on track and motivated.
- Don't hesitate to seek help from tutors or attend study groups to enhance your understanding of challenging subjects.
- Building strong relationships with professors and peers can provide valuable support and networking opportunities.

Exercise 6: Staying Safe and Legal

Objective: To ensure your safety and compliance with local laws and regulations.

Instructions:

1. Compile a list of important emergency contacts, including local authorities, your country's embassy or consulate, and university resources.
2. Research the safety guidelines and legal requirements for international students in your host country. Summarize the key points.
3. Download local safety apps that provide real-time updates on any incidents and emergency procedures.

Ming's Story: Staying Safe and Legal

"In Paris, safety was a top concern for me. I registered with the local authorities as required and downloaded several safety apps that provided real-time updates. I also made sure to keep a list of emergency contacts, including the local embassy, and learned basic French phrases for emergencies. Knowing that I had a plan in place made me feel much more secure."

Expert Insight: Ming's proactive measures in ensuring safety and compliance with legal requirements are essential practices for all international students. Registering with local authorities, using safety apps, and knowing emergency contacts can significantly enhance your safety and security. Being prepared and staying informed are key components of a safe and successful stay abroad.

Actionable Tip: Register with local authorities as soon as you arrive. Download safety apps and familiarize yourself with emergency procedures. Keep a list of important contacts and learn basic phrases in the local language for emergencies.

By sharing these stories and insights, you can see that many of the challenges you may face have been successfully navigated by others before you. Embrace the journey, seek out resources, and don't be afraid to ask for help. Your time as an international student is an adventure that will shape you in countless positive ways. Enjoy every moment and make the most of this incredible experience!

Reflection Questions:

How does having a list of emergency contacts provide you with a sense of security?

_____

_____

_____

_____

_____

_____

What are the most critical safety guidelines you need to follow in your host country, and how will you ensure you adhere to them?

_____
_____
_____
_____
_____
_____

How will staying informed about local laws and regulations impact your overall experience as an international student?

_____
_____
_____
_____
_____
_____

Additional Insights:

- Being prepared with emergency contacts and safety apps can significantly enhance your sense of security.
- Understanding and following local laws is crucial for maintaining your visa status and avoiding legal issues.
- Regularly staying informed about safety and legal requirements ensures a smooth and trouble-free stay.

Exercise 7: Exploring and Enjoying Your New Home

Objective: To fully immerse yourself in your new environment and enjoy the unique experiences it offers.

Instructions:

1. Create a bucket list of places to visit and activities to try in your host country. Prioritize them based on your interests.
2. Plan a day trip to explore a nearby city or natural attraction. Outline your itinerary and any preparations you need to make.

3. Try a new local dish each week and learn about its cultural significance.

Reflection Questions:

What are the top three places or activities on your bucket list, and what excites you about them?

_____

_____

_____

_____

_____

_____

How will planning and participating in local trips enhance your understanding and appreciation of your host country?

_____

_____

_____

_____

_____

_____

Reflect on a recent outing or trip. What did you learn or experience that deepened your connection to your home?

_____

_____

_____

_____

_____

_____

Additional Insights:

- Embrace the opportunity to explore and discover the hidden gems of your host country.
- Balancing academic responsibilities with exploration and leisure activities can lead to a more fulfilling experience.
- Trying new foods and learning about their cultural significance can be a delicious and educational way to immerse yourself in the local culture.

Chapter 4: Academic and Social Integration

Exercise 1: Understanding the Academic System

Objective: To help students familiarize themselves with the academic structure and expectations of their host university.

Instructions:

1. Research the academic system of your host university. Identify key differences between your home country's system and the new system.
2. Create a comparison chart that highlights differences in grading scales, course structures, and key academic dates.
3. Write a short reflection on how these differences might affect your study habits and academic performance.

Ana's Story: Adapting to New Academic Expectations in Germany

"When I first started my exchange program in Germany, I was overwhelmed by the different academic expectations. In my home country, the education system focused more on continuous assessment through assignments and projects. However, in Germany, the emphasis was on final exams and independent study. This shift required me to adapt my study habits significantly. I had to learn how to manage my time effectively and develop new strategies for retaining information." – Ana, Exchange Student in Germany

Expert Insight: Understanding and adapting to different academic systems is crucial for success. In countries like Germany, where final exams play a significant role, it's important to develop effective study strategies and manage your time efficiently. Seek advice from local students or academic advisors to understand what is expected. Using resources like libraries and study groups can also help you adjust to the new academic environment.

Actionable Tip: Create a study schedule that allocates time for reviewing each subject well before the exam period. Use techniques such as summarizing notes, creating mind maps, and practicing past exam papers to enhance your retention and understanding of the material. Don't forget to take regular breaks to avoid burnout—studying effectively is about quality, not just quantity.

Reflection Questions:

What are the major differences between your home and host academic systems?

_____

_____

_____

_____

_____

_____

How do you plan to adapt your study habits to fit the new academic structure?

_____

_____

_____

_____

_____

_____

What resources can you use to help understand and navigate the new system?

_____

_____

_____

_____

_____

_____

Additional Insights:

- Familiarizing yourself with the new academic system can significantly reduce academic stress. Engage with academic advisors and fellow students to gain deeper insights and practical tips on thriving in your new environment.

Exercise 2: Building Relationships with Professors and Academic Staff

Objective: To encourage students to build meaningful relationships with their professors and academic mentors.

Instructions:

1. Identify three professors or academic staff members whose courses or research interests align with your academic goals.
2. Attend their office hours and prepare a list of questions or topics to discuss.
3. Write a summary of each meeting, noting key takeaways and how you can apply their advice to your studies.

Tom's Experience: Building Relationships with Professors in Japan

"In Japan, I initially found it challenging to build relationships with my professors because of the cultural differences. However, I learned that attending office hours and showing genuine interest in their research helped me connect with them. This not only improved my understanding of the coursework but also opened up opportunities for research projects. The professors were very approachable once I took the first step." – Tom, Exchange Student in Japan

Expert Insight: Building relationships with professors can enhance your academic experience and open doors to new opportunities. In cultures where respect and hierarchy are emphasized, such as in Japan, showing interest and attending office hours can demonstrate your dedication and respect. Don't be afraid to ask questions and seek feedback—professors appreciate engaged and motivated students.

Actionable Tip: Prepare thoughtful questions related to the coursework or the professor's research before attending office hours. This shows that you are genuinely interested and have put in the effort to understand the material. Building a rapport with your professors can lead to valuable mentorship and networking opportunities.

Reflection Questions:

What steps will you take to prepare for your meetings with professors?

_____

_____

_____

_____

_____

_____

How will these interactions help you understand your coursework better or guide your academic journey?

_____

_____

_____

_____

_____

_____

What follow-up actions can you take to maintain these relationships?

_____

_____

_____

_____

_____

_____

Additional Insights:

- Building relationships with professors can provide valuable mentorship and networking opportunities. Show genuine interest in their work and seek their guidance on academic and professional matters.

Exercise 3: Effective Study Habits and Time Management

Objective: To develop effective study habits and time management skills tailored to the new academic environment.

Instructions:

1. Create a weekly study schedule that balances your academic, social, and personal activities.
2. Implement active learning techniques such as summarizing notes, using flashcards, or participating in study groups.
3. Reflect on your study habits at the end of each week and adjust your schedule as needed.

Luis' Journey: Mastering Time Management in Canada

"Balancing my studies and social life was a challenge during my exchange in Canada. I realized early on that I needed to improve my time management skills. Using a planner and setting realistic goals each week helped me stay on top of my academic responsibilities while still enjoying my time with friends. This approach prevented me from feeling overwhelmed and allowed me to enjoy my exchange experience to the fullest." – Luis, Exchange Student in Canada

Expert Insight: Effective time management is key to balancing academic and social life. Use tools like planners, digital calendars, and to-do lists to organize your tasks and commitments. Set achievable goals and prioritize your workload to avoid last-minute stress. Remember to allocate time for relaxation and social activities to maintain a healthy balance.

Actionable Tip: At the start of each week, list your priorities and deadlines. Break down larger tasks into smaller, manageable steps and allocate specific times for each activity. Review your progress regularly and adjust your schedule as needed. Make sure to include time for hobbies and socializing to keep yourself balanced and happy.

Reflection Questions:

What study techniques have you found most effective and how will you apply them in the new academic environment?

_____
_____
_____
_____
_____
_____

How will you balance your study time with social and personal activities?

_____
_____
_____
_____
_____
_____

What challenges have you faced in managing your time, and how did you overcome them?

_____
_____
_____
_____
_____
_____

Additional Insights:

- Effective time management is crucial for academic success and personal well-being. Regularly reviewing and adjusting your study schedule can help you stay on track and maintain a healthy balance between your responsibilities and leisure activities.

Exercise 4: Navigating Campus Life

Objective: To help students become familiar with campus resources and integrate smoothly into campus life.

Instructions:

1. Take a campus tour and note down key locations such as libraries, study areas, cafeterias, and health centers.
2. Attend an orientation session or campus event to meet fellow students and learn more about available resources.
3. Write a brief report on the resources you discovered and how you plan to utilize them.

Raj's Exploration: Discovering Extracurricular Activities in Australia

"I joined the university's photography club during my exchange in Australia. It was a fantastic way to explore the country and meet people with similar interests. Through club outings and events, I developed my photography skills and built a strong network of friends. It made my time in Australia more fulfilling and gave me a creative outlet." – Raj, Exchange Student in Australia

Expert Insight: Joining clubs and extracurricular activities can significantly enhance your exchange experience. These activities provide opportunities to pursue your interests, develop new skills, and meet like-minded individuals. Look for clubs and organizations that align with your passions and be proactive in participating in events and activities.

Actionable Tip: Explore the list of clubs and societies offered by your host university early in your exchange. Attend introductory meetings or events to find out which clubs resonate with your interests. Don't hesitate to try something new—you might discover a new passion. Extracurricular activities are also a great way to meet people and make lasting friendships.

Reflection Questions:

What campus resources do you find most useful, and why?

_____
_____
_____
_____
_____
_____

How can these resources support your academic and personal needs?

_____
_____
_____
_____
_____
_____

What steps can you take to become more involved in campus life?

_____
_____
_____
_____
_____
_____

Additional Insights:

- Utilizing campus resources can greatly enhance your university experience. Whether it's academic support, health services, or recreational facilities, knowing what's available and how to access these resources can help you feel more connected and supported.

Exercise 5: Social Integration and Building Relationships

Objective: To foster social connections and ease cultural adjustment in a new environment.

Instructions:

1. Join at least two student organizations or clubs that interest you.
2. Participate in social events and activities organized by these groups.

3. Reflect on your experiences and how they have helped you integrate socially.

Emily's Adventure: Social Integration and Cultural Adjustment in Spain

"During my exchange in Spain, integrating socially was initially tough due to the language barrier. I joined a language exchange program where I taught English and learned Spanish from local students. This not only improved my language skills but also helped me make friends and understand the local culture better. Being part of the community made my experience much richer and more enjoyable." – Emily, Exchange Student in Spain

Expert Insight: Language exchange programs are excellent for improving language skills and integrating socially. Participating in these programs allows you to practice the local language in a real-world context and build meaningful relationships. Additionally, engaging in cultural activities and showing interest in local traditions can enhance your cultural understanding and help you feel more at home.

Actionable Tip: Join language exchange programs or conversation clubs at your host university. Attend local events and festivals to immerse yourself in the culture and practice your language skills in various social settings. The more you engage with the local community, the more enriching your experience will be.

Reflection Questions:

What activities or clubs have you joined, and why?

_____
_____
_____
_____
_____
_____

How can these experiences help you build relationships and understand the local culture better?

_____
_____
_____
_____
_____
_____

What strategies could you use to overcome any social or cultural challenges?

_____

_____

_____

_____

_____

_____

Additional Insights:

• Social integration is essential for a fulfilling exchange experience. Actively participating in student organizations and social events can help you build a diverse network of friends and feel more at home in your new environment.

Exercise 6: Extracurricular Activities and Hobbies

Objective: To explore and engage in extracurricular activities that enrich the university experience.

Instructions:

1. List at least three extracurricular activities or hobbies you are interested in pursuing.
2. Attend introductory sessions or meetings for these activities.
3. Write a reflection on how these activities contribute to your personal growth and enjoyment.

Reflection Questions:

What new activities or hobbies have you explored, and what do you enjoy about them?

_____

_____

_____

_____

_____

How do these extracurriculars balance your academic responsibilities and enhance your academic experience?

_____

_____

_____

_____

_____

_____

What skills or lessons have you learned through these activities?

_____

_____

_____

_____

_____

_____

Additional Insights:

- Engaging in extracurricular activities can provide a break from academic pressures and help you develop new skills and interests. It's a great way to meet people, learn something new, and make the most of your time at university.

Exercise 7: Networking and Professional Development

Objective: To build a professional network and develop career-related skills.

Instructions:

1. Attend a career fair or networking event organized by your university.
2. Prepare a professional resume and practice your elevator pitch.
3. Write a summary of the event, including new contacts made and insights gained.

Reflection Questions:

How did you prepare for the career fair or networking event?

_____

_____

_____

_____

_____

_____

What were the key takeaways from your interactions with professionals and recruiters?

_____

_____

_____

_____

_____

_____

How do you plan to follow up and maintain the connections you made?

_____

_____

_____

_____

_____

_____

Additional Insights:

- Networking is an essential skill for career development. Attending career fairs and networking events provides opportunities to connect with professionals, learn about job opportunities, and receive valuable career advice. Following up with contacts and maintaining these relationships can open doors to future opportunities.

Exercise 8: Maintaining Health and Wellbeing

Objective: To prioritize physical and mental health while balancing academic and social life.

Instructions:

1. Create a self-care plan that includes regular exercise, healthy eating, and mental health practices.
2. Identify and utilize campus health services and resources.
3. Reflect on how maintaining your health and wellbeing has impacted your overall exchange experience.

Maria's Wellbeing: Maintaining Health and Wellbeing in the UK

"During my exchange in the UK, I struggled with the gloomy weather and homesickness. I found that maintaining a regular exercise routine and exploring the beautiful parks helped lift my spirits. Additionally, attending counseling sessions at the university's health center provided valuable support during tough times. Taking care of my mental and physical health made a huge difference in my overall experience." – Maria, Exchange Student in the UK

Expert Insight: Maintaining your health and wellbeing is essential for a positive exchange experience. Regular exercise, healthy eating, and mental health support can help you cope with stress and homesickness. Utilize campus health services and seek counseling if needed. Exploring your surroundings and staying active can also boost your mood and overall well-being.

Actionable Tip: Incorporate regular physical activity into your routine, whether it's joining a gym, participating in sports, or exploring local parks. Make use of mental health resources provided by your university and create a self-care plan that includes activities you enjoy and that help you relax. Staying physically active and mentally healthy will enhance your ability to enjoy and succeed in your exchange experience.

By learning from the experiences of former exchange students and following expert insights, you can navigate the challenges of your exchange program more effectively. Remember, each experience is unique, and the key is to remain adaptable, open-minded, and proactive in making the most of your time abroad. Your journey will be filled with opportunities for growth, new friendships, and unforgettable memories. Take each challenge as a learning experience and each new opportunity as a step towards personal growth.

Reflection Questions:

What self-care practices have you incorporated into your routine, and how have they helped you?

_____

_____

_____

_____

_____

_____

How do you balance your physical and mental health with academic and social commitments?

_____

_____

_____

_____

_____

_____

What resources or support systems have you found most helpful in maintaining your wellbeing?

_____

_____

_____

_____

_____

_____

Additional Insights:

- Prioritizing your health and wellbeing is fundamental to a successful exchange experience. Regular exercise, healthy eating, and mental health practices can enhance your resilience and ability to cope with challenges. Utilize available resources and create a balanced routine that supports your overall health.

Chapter 5: Cultural Immersion and Adaptation

Exercise 1: Understanding Cultural Differences

Objective: To develop an awareness of cultural differences and how they impact behavior and communication.

Instructions:

1. Reflect on a recent interaction where you noticed cultural differences. Describe the interaction in detail.
2. Identify the specific cultural norms or values that were different from your own. How did these differences influence the interaction?
3. Research and write a brief summary of three key cultural dimensions (e.g., individualism vs. collectivism, high-context vs. low-context communication) and how they apply to your host country.
4. Discuss how understanding these cultural dimensions can help you navigate future interactions more effectively.

Elena's Story: Embracing the Siesta in Spain

When Elena first arrived in Spain, she was excited but also nervous about the cultural differences. One of the biggest adjustments was understanding the concept of the "siesta." Shops and businesses closed for several hours in the afternoon, which initially felt like a disruption to her day. However, she soon realized this break was an opportunity to relax and recharge, making her evenings more enjoyable and productive. Embracing this new rhythm helped Elena appreciate the local lifestyle and integrate better into the community.

Expert Insight - Adapting to New Rhythms: Elena's experience with the siesta teaches us the importance of adapting to new daily rhythms. It's not just about adjusting your schedule; it's about understanding the cultural significance behind these practices. By embracing the siesta, Elena didn't just fit in better; she experienced the local lifestyle more fully, which enriched her stay.

Adapting to different cultural norms, like the siesta in Spain, can be challenging but also enriching. Embrace these differences as opportunities to learn and grow. Understanding and respecting local customs not only helps you fit in better but also allows you to experience the culture more authentically. Take time to observe and participate in local practices; these adjustments can enhance your overall experience.

Reflection Questions:

What were your initial reactions to the cultural differences you observed?

_____

_____

_____

_____

_____

_____

How did the differences impact your behavior or perceptions during the interaction?

_____

_____

_____

_____

_____

_____

How can you apply your understanding of cultural dimensions to improve your intercultural communication skills?

_____

_____

_____

_____

_____

_____

Additional Insights:

- Understanding cultural differences is crucial for effective communication and integration. By recognizing and respecting these differences, you can build stronger relationships and avoid misunderstandings. Continuous learning and reflection on cultural dimensions will enhance your adaptability and cultural competence.

Exercise 2: Improving Language Skills

Objective: To enhance your language proficiency and communication skills in the host country's language.

Instructions:

1. Set specific language learning goals for the next month (e.g., mastering a set of vocabulary, improving pronunciation, engaging in a conversation).
2. Choose at least two language learning resources (e.g., apps, online courses, language exchange partners) and create a weekly practice schedule.
3. Document your progress and challenges in a language learning journal.
4. Practice speaking with locals and note any new phrases or corrections they offer.

Max's Story: Overcoming Language Barriers in Japan

Max arrived in Japan with basic Japanese skills but quickly found that conversations often went beyond his comprehension. To overcome this, he joined a language exchange group where he helped locals practice English while they helped him with Japanese. This not only improved his language skills but also led to meaningful friendships. One of his most memorable experiences was learning to write calligraphy with his language partner, deepening his appreciation for Japanese culture.

Expert Insight - Language and Cultural Exchange: Max's journey highlights the power of language exchange. It's not just about learning words and grammar; it's about building bridges between cultures. By engaging in language exchange, Max formed meaningful friendships and gained deeper cultural insights, showing how language is a gateway to understanding and connection.

Overcoming language barriers is a common challenge for exchange students. Joining language exchange groups is an effective way to improve your language skills while building connections. Practice regularly, be patient with yourself, and don't be afraid to make mistakes. Immersing yourself in cultural activities related to the language, like calligraphy in Japan, can also enhance your learning experience and foster a deeper connection with the culture.

Reflection Questions:

What language learning strategies have been most effective for you?

_____

_____

_____

_____

_____

How can improving your language skills impact your interactions and experiences?

_____

_____

_____

_____

_____

_____

What challenges have you encountered, and how did you overcome them?

_____

_____

_____

_____

_____

Additional Insights:

- Language proficiency is key to deeper cultural immersion. Regular practice, setting achievable goals, and engaging with native speakers will accelerate your learning. Embrace mistakes as learning opportunities and celebrate your progress.

Exercise 3: Participating in Local Festivals and Traditions

Objective: To engage actively in local cultural events and traditions, enhancing your cultural understanding and integration.

Instructions:

1. Research upcoming local festivals, events, or traditions in your host community.
2. Choose one event to attend and prepare by learning about its significance and customs.
3. Participate fully in the event, observing and engaging with the local practices.
4. Write a reflective journal entry about your experience, including your feelings, observations, and any new insights gained.

Priya's Story: Participating in the Holi Festival in India

Priya's most unforgettable experience during her exchange in India was attending the Holi festival. The vibrant colors, music, and joyful atmosphere were unlike anything she had ever seen.

Initially hesitant to participate fully because she didn't know the customs, Priya's host family encouraged her to join in and explained the festival's significance. By the end of the day, she was covered in colors and filled with a sense of belonging and happiness.

Expert Insight - Immersing in Local Festivals: Priya's participation in Holi demonstrates the joy and learning that comes from immersing yourself in local festivals. These events are more than celebrations; they are windows into the heart of a culture. Priya's initial hesitation turned into a profound sense of belonging, illustrating the transformative power of fully engaging with local traditions.

Participating in local festivals and cultural events is a fantastic way to immerse yourself in the host culture. These events provide insights into the community's values, traditions, and social life. Don't hesitate to join in and experience these moments fully. Ask locals about the significance of the celebrations and follow their lead to ensure respectful participation. Such experiences can create lasting memories and a deeper appreciation for the culture.

Reflection Questions:

How did participating in the local event enhance your understanding of the host culture?

_____

_____

_____

_____

_____

What were the most memorable aspects of the event, and why?

_____

_____

_____

_____

_____

How did this experience change your perspective on the local community?

_____

_____

_____

_____

_____

Additional Insights:

- Engaging in local festivals and traditions provides firsthand insights into the host culture's values and social dynamics. These experiences foster a sense of belonging and enrich your cultural journey. Approach each event with curiosity and openness, allowing yourself to be fully immersed.

Exercise 4: Managing Homesickness and Building Connections

Objective: To develop strategies for managing homesickness and building meaningful connections in your host country.

Instructions:

1. Identify triggers of homesickness and document your feelings in a journal.
2. Create a list of comforting activities that remind you of home and incorporate them into your routine.
3. Set a goal to connect with at least three new people each week through social events, clubs, or volunteer activities.
4. Reflect on these interactions and how they help mitigate feelings of homesickness.

Carlos's Story: Dealing with Homesickness in Germany

During his first few months in Germany, Carlos struggled with homesickness. Everything felt foreign, and he missed his family and friends. To cope, he started cooking his favorite dishes from home and invited his new friends to join him. Sharing his culture helped Carlos feel more connected and less isolated. It also sparked his friends' interest in his background, leading to interesting cultural exchanges.

Expert Insight - Sharing Home Comforts: Carlos's strategy of cooking familiar dishes to cope with homesickness underscores the value of bringing a piece of home with you. This practice not only provided comfort but also facilitated cultural exchange. It's a reminder that while adapting to a new culture, maintaining ties to your own can enhance your experience and create meaningful connections.

Homesickness is a natural part of the exchange experience. Finding ways to incorporate elements of your home culture, such as cooking familiar dishes, can provide comfort and ease feelings of loneliness. Sharing these aspects with new friends not only helps you feel more at home but also fosters mutual cultural understanding and appreciation. Stay connected with loved ones through regular communication and seek out supportive communities within your host country.

Reflection Questions:

Which activities or routines may help you feel more at home in your host country?

_____

_____

_____

_____

_____

How can new connections and friendships impact your experience abroad?

_____

_____

_____

_____

_____

What strategies have you found most effective in managing homesickness?

_____

_____

_____

_____

_____

Additional Insights:

- Homesickness is a common challenge for international students, but proactive strategies can help mitigate its effects. Balancing connections to home with active engagement in your host community will enhance your sense of belonging and well-being.

Exercise 5: Reflecting on Cultural Growth and Future Opportunities

Objective: To reflect on your cultural growth and identify ways to leverage your experiences for future academic and career opportunities.

Instructions:

1. Reflect on your cultural journey and write a detailed account of your personal growth, including challenges overcome and key learning moments.
2. Identify specific skills and experiences gained that are relevant to your academic and career goals.
3. Update your resume or LinkedIn profile to highlight your international experiences and cultural competencies.
4. Research opportunities to continue cultural engagement, such as international clubs, study abroad programs, or global career paths.

Amina's Story: Balancing Cultural Identities in South Korea

In South Korea, Amina found herself constantly balancing her Nigerian heritage with the local culture. At first, she felt like she had to choose one over the other, but over time, she learned to celebrate both. Amina organized a cultural night where she shared Nigerian food, music, and dance with her Korean friends. They loved it, and it became a tradition. Embracing her cultural blend made her exchange experience richer and more fulfilling.

Expert Insight - Celebrating Dual Identities: Amina's story of balancing her Nigerian heritage with South Korean culture shows the beauty of celebrating dual identities. Rather than choosing one culture over the other, Amina created a blend that enriched her experience and those around her. This approach fosters a more inclusive environment and highlights the benefits of cultural diversity.

Balancing your home culture with your host culture can be challenging but rewarding. Embrace your unique cultural blend and find ways to share it with others. Organizing cultural events or simply sharing aspects of your heritage with new friends can enrich your experience and those around you. Celebrating your dual identity helps you maintain a connection to your roots while adapting to new cultural norms, creating a more inclusive and diverse environment.

Reflection Questions:

How can your cultural journey shape your personal and professional development?

_____

_____

_____

_____

_____

_____

What skills and experiences are you most proud of, and how can they be applied to your future goals?

_____

_____

_____

_____

_____

_____

What steps can you take to continue building on your cultural competencies after your exchange program?

_____

_____

_____

_____

_____

_____

Additional Insights:

- Your cultural experiences abroad are valuable assets for your future. Reflecting on your growth and strategically incorporating these experiences into your academic and career plans will set you apart and open new opportunities. Continue to seek out cultural engagement and leverage your unique perspective in all areas of your life.

Chapter 6: Health and Wellbeing

Exercise 1: Navigating Healthcare Abroad

Objective: To help students understand how to access and navigate healthcare systems in their host country, ensuring they are prepared for any medical needs that arise.

Instructions:

1. Research the healthcare system in your host country, including how to access services, what is covered by insurance, and how to find English-speaking doctors.
2. Create a list of important healthcare contacts, including local doctors, hospitals, and emergency services.
3. Develop a step-by-step plan for what to do in case of a medical emergency.

Maria's Story: Understanding the Local Healthcare System in Spain

When Maria first arrived in Spain for her exchange program, she was thrilled by the vibrant culture and beautiful landscapes. However, she was also apprehensive about how to manage her health in a new country. Shortly after arriving, Maria caught a severe cold and needed to see a doctor. She recalls, "I was anxious about finding the right healthcare provider and worried about the language barrier."

Maria's host university provided an orientation that included a detailed guide on how to navigate the local healthcare system. They offered a list of recommended doctors who spoke English and explained the process for using her health insurance. "Having this information upfront was a lifesaver," Maria says. "I followed the steps provided, and the experience was much smoother than I anticipated."

Expert Insight: Navigating a new healthcare system can be challenging, but preparation and using available resources can make the process more manageable. Many universities offer health services specifically designed for international students, including multilingual support and emergency assistance. Familiarize yourself with these resources as soon as you arrive.

Actionable Tip: Before you leave, research the healthcare system in your host country. Make a list of recommended healthcare providers, keep your insurance details handy, and don't hesitate to ask for help from your university's health center.

Reflection Questions:

What are the key differences between the healthcare system in your home country and your host country?

_____

_____

_____

_____

_____

_____

How confident do you feel about accessing healthcare in your host country after completing this exercise?

_____

_____

_____

_____

_____

_____

What steps will you take to ensure you have all necessary healthcare information readily available?

_____

_____

_____

_____

_____

_____

Additional Insights:

- Many universities offer health orientation sessions for international students. Attend these sessions to get detailed information and ask questions.
- Keep a personal health journal where you record any medical appointments, medications, and important health information.

Exercise 2: Maintaining Mental Health

Objective: To encourage students to identify stressors and develop strategies for maintaining their mental health while studying abroad.

Instructions:

1. Identify common stressors you might face in your host country (e.g., academic pressure, homesickness, cultural adjustment).
2. List three stress management techniques you can incorporate into your daily routine.
3. Research and list mental health resources available at your host institution and in the local community.

John's Experience: Managing Stress and Anxiety in Japan

John was excited about his year-long exchange program in Tokyo, Japan. The initial excitement soon gave way to feelings of stress and anxiety as he struggled to adapt to the demanding academic environment and cultural differences. "I started feeling overwhelmed by the coursework and the pressure to fit in," he shares.

Recognizing his struggle, John reached out to his university's counseling services. "The counselor was incredibly supportive and helped me develop strategies to manage my stress," he says. John also joined a mindfulness meditation group, which became a crucial part of his routine. "Practicing mindfulness helped me stay grounded and reduced my anxiety significantly."

Expert Insight: Mental health is an essential aspect of overall well-being, especially in a new and potentially stressful environment. Universities often provide mental health resources, including counseling services and wellness programs. Utilizing these resources can help manage stress and improve mental health.

Actionable Tip: If you feel overwhelmed, seek support from your university's counseling services. Incorporate stress management techniques such as mindfulness, exercise, and regular social activities into your daily routine.

Reflection Questions:

What are your main stress triggers, and how do they differ from those at home?

_____

_____

_____

_____

_____

_____

Which stress management techniques have you found most effective in the past, and why?

_____

_____

_____

_____

_____

_____

How can you incorporate mental health support into your weekly schedule?

_____

_____

_____

_____

_____

_____

Additional Insights:

- Regular physical activity, sufficient sleep, and a balanced diet are foundational to mental health.
- Mindfulness practices, such as meditation and deep breathing exercises, can significantly reduce stress.

Exercise 3: Adapting to Local Cuisine

Objective: To help students balance exploring local cuisine with maintaining a healthy diet.

Instructions:

1. Create a weekly meal plan that includes a mix of local dishes and familiar, healthy options.

2. Visit a local market or grocery store and make a list of healthy foods available.

3. Try cooking a local dish at home and invite friends to join you.

Sara's Journey: Balancing Nutrition in Italy

Sara was thrilled to immerse herself in Italian culture and cuisine during her exchange program. However, she quickly realized that indulging in delicious pasta and pizza every day wasn't sustainable for her health. "I loved the food, but I needed to find a balance to maintain a healthy diet," she explains.

Sara started cooking her own meals, blending local ingredients with recipes from home. She also explored local markets for fresh produce and healthy options. "Cooking became a fun way to experiment with new foods while ensuring I was eating balanced meals," she says. She also enjoyed sharing her home-cooked meals with friends, which helped her build a supportive social network.

Expert Insight: Adapting to local cuisine is a wonderful part of the cultural experience, but it's important to maintain a balanced diet. Cooking at home allows you to control your nutrition and explore local ingredients in a healthier way.

Actionable Tip: Balance indulgence with nutrition by cooking your own meals using local ingredients. Visit local markets for fresh produce and try integrating familiar healthy recipes with new flavors and ingredients from your host country.

Reflection Questions:

How does the local cuisine of your host country compare to your diet at home in terms of nutrition and variety?

_____

_____

_____

_____

_____

_____

What challenges do you anticipate in maintaining a balanced diet, and how can you overcome them?

_____

_____

_____

_____

_____

_____

How can cooking at home enhance your cultural experience and social interactions?

_____

_____

_____

_____

_____

_____

Additional Insights:

- Cooking at home not only allows you to control your diet but also helps you learn more about the local culture.
- Sharing meals with friends can be a great way to build relationships and create a supportive social network.

Exercise 4: Staying Active and Fit

Objective: To encourage students to find ways to stay physically active and maintain fitness routines while abroad.

Instructions:

1. Research and list local gyms, sports clubs, and fitness facilities available to you.
2. Set specific fitness goals for your time abroad and create a weekly exercise schedule.
3. Explore outdoor activities unique to your host country and plan to try at least one new activity.

David's Story: Embracing Outdoor Activities in New Zealand

David, an avid runner, found himself in New Zealand, surrounded by stunning natural landscapes. However, his usual routine was disrupted, and he struggled to find ways to stay active. "I missed my regular gym workouts, but I decided to embrace the outdoor opportunities available," he says.

David joined a local hiking group and started exploring the beautiful trails around his university. He also participated in university-organized outdoor activities, such as kayaking and mountain biking. "Not only did I stay fit, but I also made great friends and saw incredible places," he recalls.

Expert Insight: Staying active is vital for physical and mental health. Exploring outdoor activities is a great way to stay fit while also experiencing the natural beauty of your host country. Many universities offer organized sports and outdoor activities, which can be both fun and beneficial for health.

Actionable Tip: Look for local sports clubs or university-organized outdoor activities. Use the natural environment of your host country to stay active and explore new hobbies like hiking, biking, or water sports.

Reflection Questions:

What are your fitness goals, and how do you plan to achieve them while abroad?

_____

_____

_____

_____

_____

_____

What new physical activities are you excited to try in your host country?

_____

_____

_____

_____

_____

How can regular exercise benefit your overall exchange experience?

_____

_____

_____

_____

_____

_____

Additional Insights:

- Joining local sports teams or fitness classes can help you stay active and meet new people.
- Outdoor activities, such as hiking or biking, offer both fitness benefits and opportunities to explore your new surroundings.

Exercise 5: Managing Sleep and Jet Lag

Objective: To provide strategies for managing sleep and adjusting to new time zones.

Instructions:

1. Create a sleep schedule to follow during your first week in the host country to help adjust to the new time zone.
2. List at least three strategies to improve sleep hygiene and implement them in your daily routine.
3. Reflect on past experiences with jet lag and identify what worked well for you.

Clara's Challenge: Adjusting to a New Time Zone in Canada

Clara's excitement about studying in Canada was slightly dampened by the severe jet lag she experienced upon arrival. "I felt constantly tired and struggled to stay awake during the day," she recalls. Clara decided to tackle this by establishing a strict sleep schedule.

"I forced myself to stay awake during the day and spent time outside to get as much natural light as possible," she explains. Clara also avoided caffeine and heavy meals in the evening, which helped her adjust more quickly. "After about a week, my body clock reset, and I started feeling much better."

Expert Insight: Jet lag can significantly impact your sleep and overall well-being. To manage it effectively, gradually adjust your sleep schedule before you travel. Once you arrive, expose yourself to natural light and maintain a consistent sleep routine.

Actionable Tip: Prepare for jet lag by adjusting your sleep schedule before departure. Upon arrival, spend time outside in natural light and avoid stimulants before bedtime. Establishing a regular sleep routine can help your body adapt more quickly to the new time zone.

Reflection Questions:

What challenges do you anticipate with adjusting your sleep schedule, and how can you address them?

_____

_____

_____

_____

_____

How does adequate sleep impact your overall well-being and academic performance?

_____

_____

_____

_____

_____

_____

What new habits can you adopt to ensure better sleep quality?

_____

_____

_____

_____

_____

Additional Insights:

- Exposure to natural light during the day can help regulate your internal clock.
- Avoiding heavy meals, caffeine, and electronics before bedtime can improve sleep quality.

Exercise 6: Recognizing and Seeking Help for Substance Use

Objective: To raise awareness about the risks of substance use and encourage seeking help if needed.

Instructions:

1. Educate yourself about the signs of substance abuse and reflect on how you can recognize them in yourself or others.
2. Research the support services available at your host institution and in the local community for substance abuse.
3. Develop a personal plan for maintaining a healthy and balanced lifestyle, including steps to take if you encounter substance abuse issues.

Alex's Experience: Overcoming Alcohol Dependency in the UK

Alex enjoyed the vibrant social scene in the UK, but over time, his drinking habits escalated. "I started relying on alcohol to cope with stress and social anxiety," he admits. Realizing the problem, Alex sought help from his university's health center.

"The counselors were incredibly supportive and helped me connect with local support groups," he shares. Alex attended regular meetings and worked on building healthier coping mechanisms. "Addressing the issue was challenging, but it was crucial for my health and well-being."

Expert Insight: Substance abuse can develop gradually and have serious consequences. Recognizing the problem and seeking help early is vital. Universities offer confidential counseling and support services, which can provide the necessary assistance.

Actionable Tip: If you notice signs of substance abuse, seek help immediately. Use university counseling services and connect with support groups to address the issue. Building healthier coping strategies and seeking professional help are crucial steps towards recovery.

Reflection Questions:

How can you stay aware of your own substance use and ensure it remains healthy and balanced?

_____
_____
_____
_____
_____
_____

What strategies can you use to avoid peer pressure related to substance use?

_____
_____
_____
_____
_____
_____

How can seeking help for substance abuse positively impact your exchange experience?

_____
_____
_____
_____
_____
_____

Additional Insights:

• Awareness and early intervention are key to preventing and addressing substance abuse.

- Building a supportive network of friends and mentors can provide encouragement and accountability for maintaining a healthy lifestyle.

Chapter 7: Career Development and Networking

Exercise 1: Setting Career Goals

Objective: To help you identify and articulate your short-term and long-term career goals, and to create a practical plan to achieve them.

Instructions

1. Reflect on your interests, strengths, and aspirations. Write down three short-term and three long-term career goals.
2. For each goal, list the steps you need to take to achieve it. Include specific actions, resources, and deadlines.
3. Create a timeline for achieving these goals, marking significant milestones.

Sophie's Experience: Internships as Steppingstones

"During my exchange program in the Netherlands, I landed an internship with an environmental consultancy firm. The experience was eye-opening and allowed me to apply classroom theories to real-world projects. Initially, I was overwhelmed by the language barrier and the new work culture, but over time, I adapted and even managed to learn some Dutch. This internship not only bolstered my resume but also expanded my professional network, leading to a full-time job offer after graduation." – Sophie, American Exchange Student

Expert Insight: Internships are crucial for gaining practical experience and making industry connections. They provide an opportunity to apply what you've learned in class to real-world situations, and they help you build a network of professional contacts. When searching for internships, use platforms like LinkedIn and your university's career services. Tailor your resume and cover letter to highlight relevant skills and experiences. During the internship, be proactive, seek feedback, and network within the company. These steps can turn an internship into a valuable career opportunity.

Actionable Tip: Attend industry-specific networking events and workshops to increase your chances of finding internships. Always follow up with contacts you meet to maintain the connection.

Reflection Questions:

What are your main interests and strengths, and how do they align with your career goals?

_____

_____

_____

_____

_____

_____

What challenges might you face in achieving these goals, and how can you overcome them?

_____

_____

_____

_____

_____

_____

How can your exchange experience help you in achieving these goals?

_____

_____

_____

_____

_____

_____

Additional Insights

- Setting SMART goals (Specific, Measurable, Achievable, Relevant, Time-bound) can provide clarity and direction.
- Regularly review and adjust your goals as needed. Flexibility and adaptability are key to long-term success.

Exercise 2: Building Professional Skills

Objective: To develop and enhance essential soft and technical skills relevant to your career aspirations.

Instructions

1. Identify three soft skills (e.g., communication, teamwork, problem-solving) and three technical skills (e.g., programming, data analysis, project management) you need to develop.
2. Research and list resources such as online courses, workshops, or books that can help you improve these skills.
3. Create a personal development plan that includes regular practice and application of these skills in your daily activities.

Ahmed's Story: Networking at Career Fairs

"The career fair at my host university in Canada was an incredible opportunity. I was nervous at first, but after some preparation and practice, I approached several companies. These conversations were invaluable, providing insights into what employers are looking for and helping me secure interviews. One of these led to a summer internship, which later turned into a full-time job. The key was preparation and being genuine in my interactions." – Ahmed, Egyptian Exchange Student

Expert Insight: Career fairs are ideal for making direct connections with potential employers. They provide a unique opportunity to meet and talk to recruiters face-to-face. To make the most of career fairs, research companies beforehand, prepare a concise elevator pitch, and practice answering common questions. During the event, approach recruiters confidently, ask insightful questions, and engage in meaningful conversations. After the fair, send follow-up emails to thank recruiters for their time and express continued interest in their company.

Actionable Tip: Dress professionally and bring multiple copies of your resume. Approach recruiters with confidence and engage in meaningful conversations to leave a lasting impression.

Reflection Questions:

Which soft and technical skills are most essential for your desired career path?

_____

_____

_____

_____

_____

How can you integrate skill development into your current academic and extracurricular activities?

_____

_____

_____

_____

_____

_____

Which opportunities can you seek out during your exchange to practice and enhance these skills?

_____

_____

_____

_____

_____

_____

Additional Insights

- Participating in group projects, joining clubs, or taking on leadership roles can provide practical experience in developing both soft and technical skills.
- Consistent practice and seeking feedback are essential for skill mastery.

Exercise 3: Networking and Professional Relationships

Objective: To build and maintain a strong professional network that supports your career growth.

Instructions

1. Identify and list five networking opportunities (e.g., career fairs, conferences, seminars) you can attend during your exchange.
2. Prepare a brief self-introduction and elevator pitch to use at networking events.
3. Reach out to three professionals or alumni from your host institution and request informational interviews.

Carlos' Experience: The Impact of Mentorship

"Finding a mentor during my exchange in Australia was a turning point in my career. My mentor, an experienced industry professional, provided guidance on navigating the job market and developing my career plan. Through her network, I gained access to exclusive job openings and received advice on improving my resume and interview skills. Her support was instrumental in my securing a job at a top engineering firm." – Carlos, Brazilian Exchange Student

Expert Insight: A mentor can provide personalized advice, industry insights, and networking opportunities that can significantly impact your career. To find a mentor, look for individuals whose careers you admire and who have experience in your field. Approach them respectfully, expressing genuine interest in their work and explaining why you seek their guidance. Maintain regular communication with your mentor and be open to feedback. Show appreciation for their time and insights by acting on their advice and updating them on your progress.

Actionable Tip: Maintain regular communication with your mentor and be open to feedback. Show appreciation for their time and insights by acting on their advice and updating them on your progress.

Reflection Questions:

How can you effectively present yourself and your career goals during networking opportunities?

_____

_____

_____

_____

_____

_____

What questions will you ask during informational interviews to gain valuable insights?

_____

_____

_____

_____

_____

_____

How will you maintain and follow up with your professional contacts after networking events?

_____

_____

_____

_____

_____

_____

Additional Insights

- Networking is about building relationships, not just collecting business cards. Focus on meaningful interactions and follow-up.
- Use LinkedIn and other professional platforms to stay connected and engage with your network regularly.

Exercise 4: Gaining Work Experience

Objective: To explore and secure practical work experience through internships, part-time jobs, and volunteering.

Instructions

1. Research and list three potential internship or part-time job opportunities in your host country.
2. Prepare a tailored resume and cover letter for each opportunity.
3. Identify three volunteer organizations or community service projects that align with your career interests.

Aisha's Experience: Balancing Work and Study

"During my exchange in the UK, I took a part-time job at a local café. Balancing work with my studies was challenging, but it taught me valuable time management skills. The job also helped me build connections within the community and improve my interpersonal skills. This experience was not only financially beneficial but also enriched my overall exchange experience." – Aisha, Kenyan Exchange Student

Expert Insight: Balancing work and study requires effective time management and prioritization. Working part-time while studying can provide additional income, help you build new skills, and expand your professional network. Create a detailed schedule that allocates time for work, study, and leisure. Communicate with your employer about your academic commitments and seek flexible work arrangements when necessary. Additionally, make sure to set aside time for self-care and relaxation to avoid burnout. This balance will enhance your overall exchange experience and prepare you for future career challenges.

Actionable Tip: Use organizational tools like planners or digital calendars to keep track of your responsibilities. Make sure to set aside time for self-care and relaxation to avoid burnout.

Reflection Questions:

How does the work experience you seek align with your career goals and interests?

_____

_____

_____

_____

_____

_____

What skills and experiences do you hope to gain from these opportunities?

_____

_____

_____

_____

_____

_____

How can you balance work, study, and personal life during your exchange?

_____

_____

_____

_____

_____

_____

Additional Insights

- Gaining work experience abroad can provide unique insights and skills that are highly valued by employers.
- Volunteering not only enhances your resume but also helps you build a network and give back to the community.

Exercise 5: Professional Development Resources

Objective: To utilize available resources to support your career development and job search.

Instructions

1. List the career services and resources offered by your host institution (e.g., career counseling, job placement services, resume workshops).
2. Research and join at least two professional associations or student chapters related to your field.
3. Explore online platforms for job searching and skill development, such as LinkedIn Learning, Coursera, or industry-specific websites.

Lara's Experience: Leveraging Alumni Networks

"Connecting with alumni from my host institution in France was one of the best decisions I made. Through the alumni network, I met professionals who offered career advice and job referrals. One alum helped me secure an internship that perfectly aligned with my career goals. This network provided support and opened doors to opportunities I wouldn't have found otherwise." – Lara, South African Exchange Student

Expert Insight: Alumni networks are powerful resources for career development. Engage with alumni through university platforms, LinkedIn, and alumni events. Alumni can offer job leads, mentorship, and industry insights that are crucial for your career growth. When reaching out to alumni, be genuine and specific about what you are seeking. Maintain regular contact with your alumni network, share your achievements, seek advice, and offer support to others in the network.

Actionable Tip: Attend alumni networking events and actively participate in discussions. Follow up with alumni contacts and maintain these relationships by regularly updating them on your progress and seeking their advice.

Reflection Questions:

How can you maximize the use of career services and resources at your host institution?

_____

_____

_____

_____

_____

_____

What benefits do professional associations offer for networking and career growth?

_____

_____

_____

_____

_____

_____

How can you effectively use online platforms to enhance your skills and job prospects?

_____

_____

_____

_____

_____

_____

Additional Insights

- Regularly attending career workshops and networking events can keep you updated on industry trends and job opportunities.
- Professional associations often offer exclusive resources, events, and job listings for their members.

Exercise 6: International Career Opportunities

Objective: To explore and prepare for career opportunities in a global context.

Instructions

1. Research the job market and demand for your field in three different countries.
2. Identify language skills and cultural knowledge needed for working in these countries.
3. Connect with alumni or professionals working internationally to gain insights into the global job market.

Reflection Questions:

What are the key factors to consider when exploring international career opportunities?

_____

_____

_____

_____

_____

_____

How can you develop the necessary skills and knowledge to work in a global context?

_____

_____

_____

_____

_____

What steps can you take to build a globally competitive resume and network?

_____

_____

_____

_____

_____

Additional Insights

- International experience and cross-cultural skills are highly valued in today's job market.
- Stay informed about visa requirements and work regulations in the countries you are interested in.

Chapter 8: Returning Home and Reintegrating

Exercise 1: Preparing for Departure

Objective: To ensure a smooth and organized transition from your host country back to your home country by finalizing all academic and administrative tasks.

Instructions:

1. Create a checklist of all academic tasks to be completed before departure (e.g., final exams, returning library books, requesting transcripts).
2. List any administrative tasks that need to be done (e.g., settling fees, closing bank accounts).
3. Plan and schedule farewell events with friends, professors, and mentors.
4. Collect contact information from key individuals you want to stay in touch with.

Maria's Journey: Embracing Reverse Culture Shock and Finding New Balance

Returning to Italy after a year-long exchange in Canada, Maria was excited but soon found herself experiencing reverse culture shock. "It was strange," she recalls. "Everything felt familiar, yet I felt like a stranger in my own home. I missed the Canadian way of life, the friends I made, and even the cold winters!"

Maria's initial weeks were challenging. She felt disconnected from her old routines and found it hard to share her experiences with friends who had not been abroad. "They couldn't fully understand the impact the exchange had on me," she explains. To cope, Maria joined an online group for exchange returnees, where she found comfort in sharing stories and tips for readjusting. She also stayed engaged with Canadian culture by cooking Canadian dishes, watching Canadian films, and participating in local events related to Canada.

Expert Insight: Reverse culture shock is a common experience for returning exchange students. It can manifest as feelings of disorientation, frustration, and nostalgia for the host country. To manage reverse culture shock:

- **Stay Patient:** Understand that readjustment takes time. Allow yourself to gradually re-acclimate to your home environment.
- **Seek Support:** Connect with fellow returnees who can relate to your experiences. Online forums and local meetups can be invaluable.
- **Stay Engaged:** Maintain some of the routines or hobbies you enjoyed abroad. This can provide a sense of continuity and comfort.
- **Reflect and Share:** Journaling your thoughts and sharing your experiences with others can help you process your feelings and find common ground.

Reflection Questions:

What academic and administrative tasks do you need to complete before you leave your host country?

_____

_____

_____

_____

_____

_____

How can you effectively manage your time to ensure all tasks are completed?

_____

_____

_____

_____

_____

What are some meaningful ways you can say goodbye to the people you've met during your exchange?

_____

_____

_____

_____

_____

_____

Additional Insights:

- **Stay Organized:** Use digital tools like calendar apps or task management apps to keep track of deadlines and appointments.
- **Personal Touch:** Consider writing thank-you notes to professors and mentors who have significantly impacted your exchange experience.

Exercise 2: Coping with Reverse Culture Shock

Objective: To prepare for and effectively manage the emotional and psychological challenges associated with reverse culture shock.

Instructions:

1. Identify common symptoms of reverse culture shock you might experience upon returning home.
2. Develop a personal plan for coping with these symptoms, including support systems and activities that can help.
3. List the resources available at your home institution or local community for managing reverse culture shock.

Elena's Insight: Navigating Reverse Culture Shock with Support

Elena faced significant reverse culture shock when she returned to Mexico after a semester in South Korea. "I felt out of place," she recalls. "The pace of life and the social norms were so different from what I had gotten used to."

To cope, Elena reached out to her university's counseling services and connected with a group of fellow returnees. "Talking to others who had similar experiences was incredibly helpful," she says. "We shared coping strategies and supported each other through the transition." She also attended workshops on reverse culture shock, which provided her with practical tools and strategies to manage her readjustment.

Expert Insight: Navigating reverse culture shock requires patience and support. Here are some strategies:

- **Seek Professional Help:** Do not hesitate to access counseling services if you are struggling with the transition. Professional support can provide valuable coping strategies.
- **Connect with Peers:** Join groups or forums for returnees to share experiences and support each other.
- **Stay Active:** Engage in activities that you enjoyed abroad, such as cooking local dishes or practicing new hobbies, to maintain a sense of continuity.

- **Participate in Workshops:** Look for workshops or seminars on reverse culture shock to gain practical advice and meet others going through similar experiences.

Reflection Questions:

What are some potential challenges you might face when readjusting to your home culture?

_____
_____
_____
_____
_____
_____

How can you mentally and emotionally prepare for these challenges?

_____
_____
_____
_____
_____

Who can you turn to for support during this transition?

_____
_____
_____
_____
_____
_____

Additional Insights:

- **Stay Connected:** Keep in touch with fellow returnees who understand what you are going through.
- **Self-Care:** Make time for activities that help you relax and recharge, such as exercise, hobbies, or meditation.

Exercise 3: Reflecting on Your Experience

Objective: To reflect on the personal growth and skills gained during your exchange and document your experiences for future reference.

Instructions:

1. Write a reflective essay about your exchange experience, focusing on personal growth, new skills, and memorable moments.
2. Create a portfolio of your academic and extracurricular achievements during your exchange.
3. Consider sharing your experiences through a blog, social media, or presentations to inspire others.

Marco's Reflection: Documenting and Sharing the Exchange Experience

Marco, who spent a year in the United States, found great value in documenting his exchange journey. "I kept a detailed journal and took countless photos," he says. "When I returned to Italy, I compiled these into a blog to share my experiences."

This blog not only served as a personal reflection but also inspired others to consider exchange programs. "I received messages from students who were encouraged by my story," Marco notes. "It felt rewarding to know that my experiences could help others." He also created a video series where he shared tips and answered questions about studying abroad, which further expanded his reach and impact.

Expert Insight: Documenting and sharing your exchange journey can be incredibly rewarding. Here is how to make the most of it:

- **Keep Records:** Maintain a journal, take photos, and save mementos from your time abroad. These records will be invaluable for reflection and sharing.
- **Create Content:** Use your records to create a blog, photo album, or video series. This can serve as a personal keepsake and a source of inspiration for others.
- **Engage Others:** Share your experiences through presentations, social media, or workshops. Engaging with others can deepen your understanding and appreciation of your journey.
- **Expand Your Reach:** Consider creating multimedia content, such as videos or podcasts, to reach a wider audience and provide varied insights.

Reflection Questions:

How have you grown personally and academically during your exchange?

_____

_____

_____

_____

_____

_____

What new skills and perspectives have you gained?

_____
_____
_____
_____
_____
_____

How can you share your experiences with others to inspire and inform them?

_____
_____
_____
_____
_____
_____

Additional Insights:

- **Documenting Growth:** Regularly reflect on your experiences to gain deeper insights and appreciate your progress.
- **Sharing Impact:** Sharing your story can not only inspire others but also reinforce your learning and achievements.

Exercise 4: Applying Your Exchange Experience

Objective: To effectively integrate the skills and knowledge gained from your exchange into your academic and professional pursuits.

Instructions:

1. Update your resume and LinkedIn profile to include skills and experiences gained during your exchange.
2. Prepare specific examples of how your exchange experience has prepared you for academic and professional challenges.
3. Identify potential academic and career opportunities where you can apply your new skills and perspectives.

Leo's Experience: Leveraging Exchange Skills for Career Growth

After completing his exchange program in Japan, Leo returned to Brazil with a new perspective on his career. "The experience was transformative," he says. "I developed strong intercultural communication skills and a deep appreciation for different work ethics."

Leo made sure to highlight these skills in his job applications and during interviews. "I used specific examples of how I adapted to the Japanese work culture and collaborated on projects with local students," he shares. He also joined professional networks that included international members to continue leveraging his intercultural skills. This approach paid off when he landed a job with an international company that valued his global experience.

Expert Insight: Your exchange experience can significantly enhance your career prospects. Here is how to leverage it:

- **Highlight Skills:** Emphasize skills such as adaptability, intercultural communication, and problem-solving in your resume and interviews.
- **Provide Examples:** Use specific examples to demonstrate how your exchange experience has prepared you for professional challenges.
- **Network:** Utilize your international connections to explore job opportunities and gain insights into global career trends.
- **Continue Learning:** Stay updated with global industry trends and seek additional certifications or training that align with your international experience.

Reflection Questions:

How can you leverage your exchange experience in your future academic and professional endeavors?

_____
_____
_____
_____
_____
_____

What specific skills and experiences should you highlight on your resume and during interviews?

_____
_____
_____
_____
_____
_____

What new opportunities have emerged as a result of your exchange experience?

_____

_____

_____

_____

_____

_____

Additional Insights:

- **Highlight Specifics:** Use concrete examples to demonstrate the impact of your exchange experience in professional settings.
- **Continuous Learning:** Stay engaged with international communities and seek out ongoing learning opportunities to further develop your skills.

Exercise 5: Staying Connected

Objective: To maintain and nurture the international relationships you have formed during your exchange and stay engaged with the global community.

Instructions:

1. List the key individuals you want to stay in touch with and the best ways to communicate with them.
2. Join alumni networks and international associations related to your exchange program.
3. Plan to participate in virtual or in-person reunions and events to maintain your global connections.

Sofia's Strategy: Staying Connected and Building a Global Network

Returning to Spain from her exchange in Australia, Sofia was determined to maintain the international friendships she had formed. "We created a WhatsApp group to stay in touch," she says. "It's been wonderful to share updates and support each other, despite the distance."

Sofia also joined an alumni network for her exchange program. "This network has opened doors to new opportunities, including job offers and collaboration on projects," she explains. She took part in virtual events and webinars hosted by the alumni network, which helped her stay connected and informed about new developments in her field.

Expert Insight: Maintaining international relationships is crucial for both personal and professional growth. Here is how to do it effectively:

- **Use Technology:** Leverage social media, messaging apps, and video calls to keep in touch with friends and mentors from your host country.
- **Join Networks:** Participate in alumni networks and international associations to stay engaged and explore new opportunities.
- **Plan Reunions:** Organize or participate in reunions to maintain strong connections and revisit your shared experiences.
- **Engage Actively:** Attend virtual events, webinars, and online courses offered by your alumni network to stay connected and continue learning.

Reflection Questions:

Who are the key individuals you want to stay connected with from your exchange?

_____

_____

_____

_____

_____

_____

What are some effective ways to maintain these relationships?

_____

_____

_____

_____

_____

How can you stay engaged with the global community and continue to benefit from your international network?

_____

_____

_____

_____

_____

Additional Insights:

- **Regular Communication:** Schedule regular check-ins with friends and mentors to keep relationships strong.

- **Global Engagement:** Participate in international events and communities to stay connected and informed about global trends.

References

American Psychological Association. (2020). *Publication manual of the American Psychological Association* (7th ed.). American Psychological Association.

American Psychological Association. (n.d.). *About APA*. Retrieved from https://www.apa.org/about/

Babbel. (n.d.). *Language learning app*. Retrieved from https://www.babbel.com/

BetterHelp. (n.d.). *Online counseling*. Retrieved from https://www.betterhelp.com/

Booth, W. C., Colomb, G. G., & Williams, J. M. (2016). *The craft of research* (4th ed.). University of Chicago Press.

Calm. (n.d.). *Meditation and relaxation app*. Retrieved from https://www.calm.com/

Centers for Disease Control and Prevention. (n.d.). *Traveler's health*. Retrieved from https://wwwnc.cdc.gov/travel

Craswell, G., & Poore, M. (2011). *Writing for academic success* (2nd ed.). Sage.

College Board. (n.d.). *Education resources*. Retrieved from https://www.collegeboard.org/

Duolingo. (n.d.). *Language learning app*. Retrieved from https://www.duolingo.com/

ERIC (Education Resources Information Center). (n.d.). *ERIC - Institute of Education Sciences*. Retrieved from https://eric.ed.gov/

European Commission. (n.d.). *Erasmus+ Programme*. Retrieved from https://ec.europa.eu/programmes/erasmus-plus/

Glassdoor. (n.d.). *Company reviews and job search*. Retrieved from https://www.glassdoor.com/

Google Maps. (n.d.). *Navigation app*. Retrieved from https://www.google.com/maps

Google Scholar. (n.d.). *Google Scholar*. Retrieved from https://scholar.google.com/

Handshake. (n.d.). *Career services platform*. Retrieved from https://www.joinhandshake.com/

Headspace. (n.d.). *Mindfulness and meditation app*. Retrieved from https://www.headspace.com/

Hill, C. W. L. (2021). *International business: Competing in the global marketplace* (13th ed.). McGraw-Hill Education.

IAESTE (International Association for the Exchange of Students for Technical Experience). (n.d.). *IAESTE International*. Retrieved from https://iaeste.org/

Indeed. (n.d.). *Job search engine*. Retrieved from https://www.indeed.com/

Jackson, R., & Sørensen, G. (2016). *Introduction to international relations: Theories and approaches* (6th ed.). Oxford University Press.

JSTOR. (n.d.). *JSTOR digital library*. Retrieved from https://www.jstor.org/

LinkedIn. (n.d.). *Professional networking site*. Retrieved from https://www.linkedin.com/

Lonely Planet. (2021). *The Lonely Planet guide to the world* (13th ed.). Lonely Planet. Lonely Planet. (n.d.). *Travel guide*. Retrieved from https://www.lonelyplanet.com/

Molinsky, A. (2013). *Global dexterity: How to adapt your behavior across cultures without losing yourself in the process*. Harvard Business Review Press.

MyFitnessPal. (n.d.). *Fitness app*. Retrieved from https://www.myfitnesspal.com/

NAFSA (National Association of Foreign Student Advisers). (n.d.). *NAFSA: Association of International Educators*. Retrieved from https://www.nafsa.org/

National Center for Biotechnology Information. (n.d.). *PubMed*. Retrieved from https://pubmed.ncbi.nlm.nih.gov/

Nike Training Club. (n.d.). *Fitness app*. Retrieved from https://www.nike.com/ntc-app

Pollock, D. C., & Van Reken, R. E. (2009). *Third culture kids: Growing up among worlds* (3rd ed.). Nicholas Brealey Publishing.

Skyscanner. (n.d.). *Travel search engine*. Retrieved from https://www.skyscanner.com/

Storti, C. (2001). *The art of crossing cultures* (2nd ed.). Nicholas Brealey Publishing.

Thomas, D. C., & Inkson, K. (2017). *Cultural intelligence: Living and working globally* (3rd ed.). Berrett-Koehler Publishers.

TripAdvisor. (n.d.). *Travel platform*. Retrieved from https://www.tripadvisor.com/

TripIt. (n.d.). *Travel planning app*. Retrieved from https://www.tripit.com/

U.S. Department of State. (n.d.). *Travel.state.gov*. Retrieved from https://travel.state.gov/

Brandon Arroues, M.Ed.

Brandon Arroues is an accomplished educator and consultant with a master's degree in Instructional Design. He has earned numerous awards including the Excellence Award in Research Writing and the Excellence Award in Classroom Management, Engagement, and Motivation. As a member of Kappa Delta Pi, the International Honor Society in Education, Brandon has demonstrated a commitment to academic excellence and professional growth.

Brandon's educational journey is marked by continuous learning and research. He is actively engaged in research in educational psychology, counseling, and phenomenology, and is currently pursuing a Ph.D. in Industrial and Organizational Psychology with a focus on Evidence-based Coaching.

Brandon began his career in international education in 2013 with his first role in Shandong, China. Since then, he has had the privilege of living and working across the United States, Europe, Eastern Asia, and Southeast Asia. His extensive experience includes roles in general education, special education, administration, and counseling within the international education sector.

In 2018, Brandon founded Brilliant Consulting & Advocacy, a consultancy dedicated to supporting individuals and institutions in navigating the complexities of education and mental wellness. His work focuses on enhancing outcomes through innovative strategies and personalized support.

Brandon's passion for international education and mental wellness is driven by his belief in the transformative power of cross-cultural experiences. Through his work, he aims to empower others to embrace new challenges and grow personally, academically, and professionally.

When he is not working, Brandon enjoys exploring new cultures, engaging in research, arts and crafting, and spending time with loved ones. He is always eager to connect with readers and fellow educators to share insights and foster a global community of learning.

www.ingramcontent.com/pod-product-compliance
Lightning Source LLC
Chambersburg PA
CBHW082111120626
46553CB00011B/3628